To Reach the Stars

By
Teresa E. Garvin

Teresa E. Garvin

Teresa was born and raised in Poland and immigrated to the U.S.A in 1979. She began her first business only two years after moving to the States. In the following years she has been ultra successful in starting several small businesses. Currently she is the founder and CEO of two separate entities, Real Estate Investment Co. and Clean Impressions Corp.

Creating value and making clients happy has always been a priority for Teresa and she prides herself on the quality of service her clients receive.

Teresa is a huge advocate of women's financial independence. She has received recognition as an Ambassador of Women Entrepreneurship. She is a successful woman with a desire to share her experience and inspire others.

Copyright © 2018 Teresa E. Garvin. All rights reserved.

No part of this publication may be reproduced, distributed, or transmitted in any form or by any means, including photocopying, recording, or other electronic or mechanical methods, without the prior written permission of the publisher, except in the case of brief quotations embodied in reviews and certain other non-commercial uses permitted by copyright law.

ISBN:
ISBN-13:

Dedication

I dedicate this short story to my loving husband that without him and his love, my life would take totally different shape. I remain forever Grateful that he is in my life.

Contents

Foreword 1

Chapter One 3

Chapter Two 5

Chapter Three 9

Chapter Four 13

Chapter Five 19

Chapter Six 23

Chapter Seven 27

Foreword

This is a short story I wrote as a contributing author to "Business Inspirations" which was a joint effort of 20 successful Polish women from different parts of the world written to share business inspirations and inspire other women to build their own financial independence.

"Business Inspirations" was an opportunity to share the "real life" experience I have gained from starting and running a few companies over the past 37 years in the USA.

The original book consisted of 20 chapters, and thus 20 women. I mention this book on my website; and although it is not currently available for sale, if you want a copy, let me know through correspondence and I will try to get a printed version sent to you. The book was published in two languages: Polish and English.

The story you have in your hands is the original version of the story I wrote for "Business Inspirations". I decided to write a just a fragment of my biography to give you a sense of the reality of what the life of an immigrant in a new country looked like.

For all of you who live in another country other than the one in which you were raised, you may find a lot in common with some of the situations I encountered. For those who have never left their country, this story can help you understand how lucky you are that you did not have to miss your friends, family, known places from childhood and finally your country.

Everything you read here is true, I started with nothing in the US; and with a lot of effort and determination I dared to dream and live an American dream in its full color.

I hope you will like it!

I hope that it will inspire you!

It's for your SUCCESS!

Chapter One

"Every decision you make, no matter how small, is a step towards success or a step towards failure"

On a beautiful fall evening in 1979 I stepped off the plane at O'Hare International Airport with one suitcase, a healthy dose of courage and a dream that would take me far beyond anything I could have imagined. I was a long way from my home in Poland. Today when people think of Poland, it conjures images of beauty, stability, freedom and hope. The history of Poland though is long and intense. Wars, Coups and Communism have etched the Polish people with a resilient nature that is prevalent today. I am product of that resilience and I am forever grateful.

    I grew up in a little village outside of Sandomierz, Poland. My father was an abusive alcoholic. My mother worked two jobs trying to keep the family financially above water. Both mentally and physically absent from the home, I was placed in the role of caregiver for my younger brother, Andrew. A child myself I essentially became the "mom and dad"- cooking, cleaning and making sure homework was done.

My memories from my childhood are dark, consumed with the knowledge of instability. There were constant battles, raised voices and fights between my parents, which were not only verbal but also physical. Several times when I tried to intervene I was beaten. During each Christmas season things would always go from bad to worse. My father's birthday ironically enough was on Christmas Eve. He would return from his "celebration" incredibly drunk and incredibly abusive. Our home was not happy, but I vowed I would get through and persevere.

I finished high school and went to college in Rzeszow. During college I met my future husband and married at 21. I felt as if my life was truly beginning.

One of the only things my husband and I owned outright was a sweet Fiat 125. Please understand 1970's communist Poland limited people in harsh and controlling ways. There was little possibility to start a business or advance to a desired level of financial security. With our sweet Fiat 125 however, we decided to start a Taxi business.

We looked at the numbers and decided adding an additional car would help to accomplish our goal quickly. The best way to earn money was to actually leave Poland. So my husband and I decided I would go to the United States, work for 2 years, and by the end of my stay our "fleet" of Taxi's would be complete.

Chapter Two

Step one was to get a passport and visa. In those days however, it was a near impossible task. Fortunately, backed by great connections and a dash of luck my passport and visa became a reality.

I had heard from those who returned from the US it really was the Promised Land of opportunity. I knew this was the right decision– I must go!

And so I found myself curbside at O'Hare International in Chicago, alone but with my dream intact.

Years before I had met a woman from my college in Rzeszow who asked if I wanted to go with her to Chicago. I couldn't then, but now I was hoping she would help me. And she did. Her name was Kazia.

She helped me find a job and place to live. This was a huge help for me and a lesson that would travel with me for the rest of my life... helping others is key. As I said, I arrived in Chicago with one suitcase and the equivalent of three weeks' salary. I couldn't even speak English but my optimism was high and I was ready to accomplish my goal.

My first job was to clean households during the day. There were 10 of us who would be picked up around 6:30AM and dropped off at various client homes. At night I was cleaning offices. I remember getting scared once when I noticed blood running down the handle from my vacuum. In pain but laughing, I realized it was my blood from my blistered hands. My day would end at 1:00AM. It was extremely hard work; the "Promised Land" looked very unrealistic and quite depressing.

I longed for home. My return ticket was sitting on top of the dresser as a constant reminder I could go back at any time. But I had courage and my dream was stronger than blistered hands and a tired body. In my darkest moments, when I was in doubt I couldn't handle the crazy schedule, I created a bit of a ritual which kept me going...I would touch my suitcase and say, "Soon we will go home and all will be well."

A new day always brings new perspective, so typically by the next morning I would be more realistic knowing the amount of money we needed for our car was on track and that my two-year time limited would go quickly.

My residential/commercial cleaning job lasted about six months. From there I found a job as a babysitter/housekeeper that also lasted about six months. I was making and saving money. The goal was in sight.

One of the best things I did during my first year was to learn English. I learned English with purpose and intensity. My method of learning was neither conventional nor typical, but boy was it effective. I decided to learn by creating a story. My first story was about me, very simple. I started with my name, Teresa. Then on to where I was born and when. I continued to my mother's name and so on. Every day my story grew a little bigger and when I needed another word I just made a note in Polish and the next day, after research and translation, I replaced it with the English word. Everyday I was creating another sentence. I found this was the best way of learning a language when there was no time to go to school.

Because I was alone a lot, even on weekends, I was able to speak out loud and hear myself telling the story. It was invaluable. I could form the words and phrases in the mirror and actually hear how they sounded. It was a lonely time for me, working long hours was not conducive to making friends. But my courage and tenacity were still intact and my goal was strong.

After one year, I learned enough English to get a job with Hilton Hotels as a front office cashier. Life was looking better! I had one year to go and the money for the car was adding up.

John Lennon once said, "Life is what happens to you while you're busy making other plans." Like a sucker punch that comes from behind I received a message from home. Although in reality it was really more of a question, "Why are you buying a car for a man that is having a child with another woman? She lives in your home, she is wearing your clothes and she continues to sleep with your husband." In shock and disbelief, I refused to believe this could be true. Less than two weeks earlier I used my entire savings and borrowed an additional $500.00 because he was emphatic he needed the money immediately. The only thing left for him to do was to choose the color of the car. Could this be true? Expecting a child? No, not him. Our life, our dream gone?

Chapter Three

I had to wait another week to find out. In this modern era of cell phones, Internet and Skype it is difficult to understand the slowness of global communication, but this was Poland in 1980. A time of telegrams and stationary phones and even so not all families in Poland had access.

My father, who had never been my advocate, had become my friend. When my father went to check on the situation, he found my husband, my husband's lover and their newborn child at home, my home.

I remember as my father relayed the details to me over the phone I had the feeling I was standing on the edge of a cliff, if I made a step forward I would fall. The realization hit me, I didn't have any place to return to, and I was without a home. I was without a dream. My parents lived in this small old house built in 1927 that my father inherited from his father. My brother and his newly pregnant wife lived on the top floor. There truly was no place to go.

I remained in a state of shock for a few weeks. My courage dented, my heart, broken.

As I began to heal I came to the conclusion I had to do something other than what I was doing, something that would bring me more cash flow, more opportunity and more freedom. My first thought? Get a Green Card. My second? Start a business.

None of my friends owned a business. Their lives focused on the work they did for others and they were grateful to have the work.

I had no formal business training or education. So everyday I began brainstorming about business. What if I start a business? What business can I do? Using common sense and my intuition I started researching how to begin, even though I still had limited language skills, and no experience in business, I began with these questions:

- What do Polish people really do when they come to US?
- What is the need people have and what will they pay?
- Whom can I hire to work for me if I start a business?

During my initial research I discovered the best businesses to start could be a roofing company, masonry company, work /job placement agency or a cleaning service.

The most important criteria I found was that a business should be *Repeatable*, *Necessary* and *Sustainable*.

Repeatable- Not a one time service but services which are needed daily, weekly, annually, etc. The initial effort gets repeating results.

Necessary- In a bad economy the business will still be needed.

Sustainable - A certainty that I would not lose all my clients at once even in the hard times during an economic down turn.

The only business I found that fit the profile was cleaning service.

"When choosing your future business, consider this:
My strong belief is that you need to find something in your environment that people need and are willing to pay money for. Something that is a problem. If you find a solution for this problem, then you have a business. Sometimes you will see that the competition is already doing something, however, if you find a better solution then your competition, you have a business!
Create more value than your competition and you will have sustainable business. This is true for product or business."

Creating and running a cleaning company is not the glamorous dream most people set out to experience. It wasn't sexy but it was functional. I had found my courage again and I was ready to succeed.

As you can imagine a cleaning business was never on my dream list of professions that I wanted to do. This was a vehicle to give me financial freedom to do what I wanted to accomplish later.

"The biggest risk is not taking any risk...
In a world that is changing really quickly, the only strategy that is guaranteed to fail is not taking risks at all" -Mark Zuckerberg

When I started my first business I loved it, I had discovered the solution to my situation. I made myself a big promise... if I do this right I will become financially free. I knew I had something for women just like me coming to the US without any real grasp of the English language. I could create an environment in which they would feel honored, valued and happy to work for me. I intended to give them every reason to want to work for me.

5

"Why I am so detailed? It is my hope that this will inspire one, two or more of you who are reading this. Because if you haven't reached your goal, chances are that all you need, or all you are missing in your life is a little inspiration.

When you hear: 'Due what you love and you will become a success.' Why then, statistically do 95% of businesses close in the first 5 years from startup?

Think about how many dreams failed."

Chapter Four

I started my first business–Residential Cleaning Company in my second year of emigration. I found a way to move past the pain and methodically lay out the foundation for my future.

It wasn't easy to grow the business; there was a lot of competition. Not only was competition fierce, this again was the era, even the US, of landlines, answering machines and pagers. My skill of marketing was entirely by intuition. I was doing things that later would be re-enforced by mentors but at the time I was flying without a net and loving every minute. Years later I received conformation that my instincts and practices were spot on.

I was adding value and creating outstanding service while at the same time caring for my employees and clients. The growth factor of my business was mostly through word of mouth. I hired only the best and the best came from recommendations.

Let me give you some values I created which were intrinsic to my business:

- In the beginning when I had only one car to deliver my employees to their job site, I was the driver.
- Usually we had clients in the suburbs of Chicago. When I finished my route instead of returning to Chicago where I lived, I would choose one client each day to give them "free of charge" services. It could be as simple as planting flowers, de-cluttering the garage and house or staying with a baby for a few hours to give the client a bit free time for herself.
- For my employees, I paid slightly more than my competition and 1⁄2 day pay if I could not provide work for the day. This would insure my employees stayed with me and felt valued.

Those simple touches had big results. I experienced tons of referrals from existing clients and spectacular recommendations for new employees.

On several occasions I would receive calls from people newly immigrated to the US looking for work. My name was at the top their list. If I did not have an open position, they waited. I look back on those days fondly and with a deep sense of gratitude, knowing my intuition paved the way for success.

"When you have a business make sure you give more value than your competition is giving and your client's choice will be simple. They will choose you!"

After 5 years of paperwork, hard work and interviews, I received my *Green Card*. So much time, so much heartache, I was a long way from that young girl who stood on the curb at O'Hare International. I was divorced from my husband, leaving everything

I contributed to that marriage behind and I was in process of a church annulment. I felt free. The world was before me once again and I was standing strong. It was time to visit my homeland and my family.

My journey home would take place in August 1984. Although my growing years were dark and desperate-distance, time and tragedy have a unique way of healing wounds once thought impossible to heal. I began the process of building my parents their dream home during the spring before I arrived in Poland. This decision benefited both my parents as well as my brother, his wife and their two children.

"Living is Giving" – Anthony Robbins

The house was a great design, it allowed for two families. Each family would have a separate entrance. My goal was to get them all in by Christmas. Relying once again on my courage, intuition and power of persuasion I challenged the builder, "you make sure that this house is done the first week of December and I will pay you more than what you have agreed on with my father." It worked! My parents moved into their new home before Christmas. In addition to the home I also purchased my father his very first car. It took all of my savings, five years worth but it was absolutely wonderful. I was so happy I could change the life condition of my family, but most importantly the life of my mom.

"For those who are willing to make an effort, great miracles and wonderful treasures are in store" – Isaac Bashevis Singer

With a happy heart and a deleted saving account I headed back to the US to continue my life and business. In many respects, I was starting over. I had friends, a business, all of it but I didn't have romance. Until Paul. He came in to my life delightfully. Soon, he proposed. We were married on the Island of Kauai in the Fern Grotto. 1985 never looked so good. We purchased our first home together in Chicago. I am proud to say our relationship is 32 years strong and continues to grow daily.

In 1997 we sold our home and purchased a new home in the suburbs of Chicago. During this time my business was growing. It was not just residential, but a healthy portion was also commercial cleaning. My business consisted of 45 women cleaners, 3 drivers and me.

Owning a business in the city and living in the suburbs added quite a bit of stress. It was time to make a difficult choice. For the health of my sanity and marriage I decided to sell the residential part of my business. However, I kept the commercial part. And because of who I am, I decided to start an entirely new company.

"Find someone who you can model, get that person to help you, don't be afraid to ask questions even if the questions apply to very simple aspects of your business. You will save time and money. Don't use my old method trial and mistakes!"

After I relaxed a little and re-grouped, it was time to begin research on how to do commercial cleaning only. It was a new business and new challenges that again I had to figure out myself. I had been in this circumstance before... there was no mentor and no one to follow to copy their success. I needed to create my own path and trust my intuition. I remember clearly problems would arise, even little things and I wished that I had someone to help me. I always kept my eyes open for a mentor but was never fortunate at the time to find one.

The age of the computer dawned and I began to do my invoices and proposals in a more efficient and quicker way. It was exciting.

There was a new curve to learning; how to create letters, better my proposals, database, bookkeeping and yes, I discovered the Internet. It took me a while, but learning and research was and is a strong key to my success, so when I finally got the hang of it, I kept thinking, "How did I ever do business without this?" My first website though was a total failure! The only people who got to see my website were those who had the exact address. Ah, live and learn!

Chapter Five

My husband and I continued to live in the suburbs of Chicago. We had a new house built in a planned upscale community. We created a lifestyle that allowed us to travel to many parts of the world including back to Poland. I remember taking my husband to Warsaw, Krakow, Zakopane, Prag, Vienna, Berlin and other parts of Europe in 1987. What a different time! We fell in love with Krakow, my husband especially, with his artistic and architectural background. The city had a soul combined with excellent energy. It filled us up when we walked the beautiful streets of the historic district and we still feel those effects today.

    The same happened when we visited Zakopane. My husband was so impressed with the architecture and the hand carved art he invited the artist to our home to do some work. The artist designed a deck and carved several levels. It was admired and respected throughout our neighborhood. As we kept making changes though and improving things for our home we realized we were exceeding the property value for our community. We would definitely lose money, so we decided to sell and build our dream home somewhere else. That home however continues to hold a memory for me that I will cherish always...my parents made the trip from Poland and visited with us for several weeks.

Life was full but not complete. I had created businesses, traveled the world, had a great marriage but we desperately wanted a child. Finally I got pregnant. We were excited, hopeful and joyful. And then, we were devastated. The pregnancy failed. Through our grief and mourning we knew we were meant to have a child, to save a child. Less than two years later we decided to adopt. We connected with a Russian orphanage and our final decision was close. However, the Polish Consulate in Chicago insisted that we adopt a child from Poland.

And yes, we literally saved a child. Little Evelyn was born prematurely. She had Fetal Alcohol Syndrome and had been exposed to tuberculosis. Three Polish families refused to adopt her. At almost one year she refused eye contact with anyone, and it was reported to us she never smiled. So when she smiled for us, it was a sure sign she would become our beautiful daughter.

Her adoption, as you can imagine, was a challenge, a challenge that required our full attention.

The decision to sell my substantial business was easily made. I divided the business in three parts. Part one and two were sold to friends who had wanted to own a similar business. I remained the owner of the third part but had a trusted friend take over the day-to-day operations.

As I have learned there is never just one change in life, shortly after the sale of my business, Paul received a new job offer in Houston. We knew it was a good solid move.

Raising Evelyn was one of my greatest joys. Paul was doing well at his job and after a year of renting we purchased our home in Houston. Even though I wanted to keep Evelyn all to myself, I knew she needed contact with other children her age. It was time for her start kindergarten.

Once Evelyn began school, my entrepreneurial nature kicked in and I was ready to create. I decided my next adventure would be in real estate. I became an agent and began investing.

We had lived in Houston for three and half years. I felt at home. We had good friends, I was investing and working in real estate, our family had time to plan weekends away from home. Days were bright; life was smooth.

Calls that come in the middle of the night are never good. My father phoned on that warm evening to tell me my mother had a deadly illness. She had been diagnosed with bone cancer. My head was spinning and my heart was aching, but I knew I had to do something. I caught the first flight to Sandomierz, Poland.

"I realized then the power of being financially independent and making my own decisions"

As stood over her bed I was thankful I could be there to hold her hand and tell her how much I loved her. The doctors gave her few weeks to live at best. I decided to take her to a specialized clinic in Lublin, Poland. This clinic would administer experimental drugs that would I purchase through a special pharmacy.

Life is so, so brief. I knew I had to help her. I would have to re-organize my business and work full-time to afford all she needed. As an independent businesswoman it never crossed my mind to ask my husband to financially participate. I am sure he would have, but I knew it was my responsibility and my gift to her.

Chapter Six

I returned to the US with a plan. Although we lived and had our home in Houston, we still owned a house in Chicago. The home in Chicago was under contract to be sold but there were several contingencies. We decided Chicago was the best place to return for my business so we cut the sale off and returned to Chicago full time.

Through intense study and determination I quickly became a Real Estate Broker in Illinois. My intention was to pursue the profession fully. When I informed my previous residential and commercial clients I was back and would like to service all of their real estate needs, I discovered they missed my services and they were vocal about getting me back. My customers gave me an ultimatum, "take over the management or we will find another service." I still controlled the third part of my previous business. In a great passive income play it was generating about $2000 per month for my family. I had a decision to make.

> *"It's in your moments of decision that your destiny is shaped. Choose wisely." –Anthony Robbins*

To choose wisely you must weigh all of your options. For me, the best and most profitable option was to start another commercial cleaning company. I have owned this business for over nineteen years now. My plan is to keep a hold of it until I die. Hopefully my plan will work.

> *"Don't worry about statistics related to high probability of failure (95% businesses are closing within 5 years). I am the perfect example those statistics must be wrong."*

Several things I have learned along the way have shaped the way I do business and my thought process when evaluating my next move:

- Consider choosing something to do as business that will make you money and not something that otherwise you would consider your hobby.
- Make the business better than your competition. Add value. Innovate in your market.
- Business is nothing more than innovation and marketing.
- After you create a cash flow with your "problem solving" business, then go on and pursue your hobbies.
- Invest in something additional that you love and create additional cash flow.

To be clear, I am not snubbing those who have been successful in creating a business from their hobbies, I consider those folks extremely lucky and I say, "Congratulations!" For me though, that simply was not my path.

With the advent of my new company it was time to learn how to compete with a new generation. I had to introduce new technology in every aspect of my business. My intuition was still strong but I knew I had to learn from others. I needed to invest in new programs, hire a coach and search for a mentor. During my quest, I discovered a book, The Secret by Rhonda Byrne. Included in the book are several manifestos written by different authors. Two of the authors, Bob Proctor and John Assaraf agreed to become my mentors.

John Assaraf included me as one of fourteen companies from all over the World in a Mastermind for 6 months. I have visited his home, which is featured in his personal story of powerful visualizations. Through my years I have met many people who have had a tremendous impact on the way I do business today. My life and business are much richer because of their counsel.

I learn daily, I never stop. The realization of today, demands knowing that new technology is a must for the growth of a business and your own personal growth. There is always another level.

As my business started to succeed and my mentors were in place, I continued to visit Poland on regular basis. I made sure my mom was well cared for and I did everything possible to accommodate her needs.

Chapter Seven

In 2005, I was sitting at a party with many of my Polish women friends. For years I had been using a visualization method I learned from my mentor, John Assaraf. So, during the party, my friends and I began to dream. We talked about our visits to Poland... where we stay, where we rent a car and what cities we like to visit. It all started with just an idea. We thought, "How wonderful would it be to have an apartment in Poland. Full of everything you could possibly need in order to no longer carry luggage or rent a car... simply own the car outright." I could completely visualize the sensation of jumping on a plane, any time I desired, carrying only a handbag and fly to Europe. I liked the idea so much that I said we should do it! After thinking and planning a bit more I added only a few requirements...it must be newly built, a security guarded building, an onsite gym and an underground garage. I gave myself two years to accomplish this. I loved the idea so much; I continued to add details each day in my imagination to make the dream even more real.

One year later we decided the location for our future "Base in Europe" would be Krakow. The city still held my heart, so full of energy and exquisite design. We placed the down payment on a new build and in September 2009 we officially had our basecamp.

"Don't be afraid to dream big! Don't limit your ability of crystalize your goals by thinking that you can't do it."

We shipped all furniture and necessities including a car from the US. The dream became reality. I am able to travel two to four times per year for two to four weeks at a time. When we travel to Europe now, there is not much planning. The location and amenities in our building exceeded our expectations. It is exactly how I visualized this dream.

"Dream big! Make a blue print; follow the steps to get you to your goal. Have patience, perseverance and believe."

As my commercial cleaning business continued to grow, I also maintained my Real Estate Broker license. My husband and I created a real estate investment portfolio. Armed with more education in real estate and the brutal economic instability of the world, we continue to change and modify to meet our needs for a secure retirement. None of this would have been possible without courage, perseverance, intuition and mentors.

My list of mentors is long, however I will mention only a few- Don Kennedy, Rich Scheferen, Mike Koenigs, Brian Tracy, Eben Pagan, Dean Graziosi, and my greatest inspiration and mentor - Anthony Robbins.

In 2015, I became a Platinum Partner with the Tony Robbins Institute.

I was honored to attend the following workshops: Life Mastery, Business Mastery, Financial Mastery, and Leadership Academy.

I have learned incredible principles and life changing lessons:

- *If you find a Mentor – someone who did this before – you will save years of time and tons of money for omitting the trial and mistake period, like I did.*
- *Don't have a Mentor? Hire a coach/ mentor who "Walked the Walk" and not just someone who learned in theory how is it done. With the information overload that we have right now, you can find it yourself online.*
- *Be different, be determined and become resistant to small roadblocks in your way.*
- *Remember, in moments of your decisions you are shaping your future.*
- *Don't be afraid to join networking sessions, meetings and events.*
- *Participate and ask qualifying questions that would bring you one step closer to the clarity of how to do your business.*
- *Don't get discouraged when you hear something again on a topic – remember, "Repetition is the mother of skills."*
- *Don't forget to buy insurance for your business – this is a protective expense- it's a must!*
- *Get basic knowledge regarding taxes and bookkeeping. Plan for two to three years in advance how on operating your business. "Success Leaves Clues" –Anthony Robbins*

Today we have cell phones, computers, Internet, loads of information at our fingertips. These are the things not even Kings and Queens had fifty years ago. We are rich. We must use these things to grow, create and dream.

Did you know that growth is one of six human needs? We must experience growth to thrive.

Ask yourself, what do you want in life? Whatever it is you want, study it. If you want love, study relationships. If you want money, study business.

If you want wealth, study wealth and so on. Get each of the best in everything-best coach, best mentor, best tools, best strategy, best map that will get you from where you are now to where you want to be. Find out what they are doing and save years of frustrations and money.

Today I am financially independent and on my way to absolute financial freedom. I am busy automating my business in such way I can be involved from any place in the world, at any time. Going forward, I am creating a new business as a Consultant. I am also starting a new charitable organization. This organization will help young adults to furnish their own apartment after leaving their life in an orphanage.

I fly in and out O'Hare International often. I always pause to remember that lonely girl who came with just one suitcase, a healthy dose of courage and a dream. Life could have been much different, maybe it would have been easier, who knows? But what I do know is that I started from nothing and I now live the American Dream...in full color. You can too. Listen to me now and I promise, you will thank me later.

Printed in Great Britain
by Amazon